GINGERBREAD GEMS

VICTORIAN ARCHITECTURE OF CAPE MAY

Schiffer Publishing Ltd

4880 Lower Valley Road, Atglen, PA 19310 USA

TINA SKINNER

PHOTOGRAPHY BY BRUCE WATERS

Library of Congress Cataloging-in-Publication Data

Skinner, Tina.
Gingerbread gems: Victorian architecture of
Cape May / by Tina Skinner;
Bruce Waters, photographer.
p. cm.
ISBN 0-7643-1971-X (pbk.)
1. Architecture--New Jersey--Cape May--
Pictorial works. 2. Architecture, Victorian--New
Jersey--Cape May--Pictorial works. I. Title.
NA735.C32 S59 2004
720'.9749'98'--dc22
2003022964

Designed by Bonnie M. Hensley
Cover design by Bruce Waters
Type set in Zurich Cn BT

ISBN 0-7643-1971-X
Printed in China

Published by Schiffer Publishing Ltd.
4880 Lower Valley Road
Atglen, PA 19310
Phone: (610) 593-1777; Fax: (610) 593-2002
E-mail: Info@schifferbooks.com

For the largest selection of fine reference books
on this and related subjects, please visit our
web site at **www.schifferbooks.com**
We are always looking for people to write
books on new and related subjects. If you have
an idea for a book please contact us at the
above address.

This book may be purchased from the publisher.
Include $3.95 for shipping.
Please try your bookstore first.
You may write for a free catalog.

In Europe, Schiffer books are distributed by
Bushwood Books
6 Marksbury Ave.
Kew Gardens
Surrey TW9 4JF England
Phone: 44 (0) 20 8392-8585;
Fax: 44 (0) 20 8392-9876
E-mail: info@bushwoodbooks.co.uk
Free postage in the U.K., Europe; air mail at cost.

PREFACE

Dear Reader,

We've worked hard to double check facts, dates, and names, and hope you will help us. Please forward any errors or ommissions in writing so that we might incorporate these changes into our next edition. Thank you for your support.

The Author & Editors

INTRODUCTION

As the first and oldest shore resort in the United States, the pretty little town of Cape May still draws an estimated twenty million visitors annually. They come for the beautiful beaches, the cool air from both ocean and bay, to marvel at migratory birds by the horde, and to absorb the history. Today, this National Historic Landmark City offers fine beaches, exciting restaurants, and tree-shaded streets lined with Victorian homes and shops. In all, more than 600 restored Victorian structures stand in this petite city, all easily accessed by a day's walk.

Wealthy and middle-class vacationers began flocking to the peninsula in the early 1800s. They journeyed from Philadelphia, Delaware, Maryland, Virginia, New York, and throughout Pennsylvania and New Jersey. Ships carrying goods from the Southern states also carried planters' families and dropped them off at Cape May on the way out, picking them up on the return trip. The social elite of Philadelphia and Delaware deemed it the "in" place to go, and it rivaled Newport, Rhode Island, and Saratoga Springs, New York, as the summer destination of choice. Among the rich, powerful, and famous who found themselves in Cape May were U.S. Presidents Franklin Pierce, Chester A. Arthur, Ulysses S. Grant, and Benjamin Harrison. Philadelphia department store magnate and U.S. Postmaster General John Wanamaker had a cottage in Cape May. Actress Lily Langtry, writer Bret Harte, American Red Cross founder Clara Barton, Mexican Empress Carlotta, and Wallis Warfield, later the Duch-

Tina Skinner

809 Kearney Avenue. Modest touches of gingerbread under the cornice returns allow the pinstripe painting to stand out on brackets.

ess of Windsor, all visited. Composer John Philip Sousa marched his band on the lawn of Congress Hall and automotive leaders Louis Chevrolet and Henry Ford vied with others to win a car race on the beach in 1905.

A major fire destroyed thirty-five acres of Cape May's wooden architecture in 1878. The town was rebuilt, most in the fanciful, ornamented styles that typified the time and attract people to Victorian style today. Three famous architects played a leading role in the rebuilding: Frank Furness, Samuel Sloan, and Stephen Decatur Button. Their talents, paired with the timely invention of the jigsaw, saw heavily ornamented cottages and mansions spring up in a small space and time frame in the city.

But the newly rebuilt town was falling out of favor. Atlantic City, further up the coast, was thriving. The town started to make a comeback after World War II, when most Americans invested in a car. Then, in 1967, the city undertook it's Victorian District Urban Renewal Project, tearing down hopelessly dilapidated structures and giving the rest a new lease on life. The town was designated a "Historic District" on the National Register of Historic Places in 1976, ready to deliver when the Americans became enamored with all things Victorian in the 1980s.

The Sea Mist, 927 Beach Avenue. Acres of railing add fantasy and secluded viewpoints for guests.

The Brass Bed Inn, 719 Columbia Avenue, c. 1872. Gothic Revival with bump-out sunroom over flat veranda roof. The earth tone pigments – high-gloss and matte yellow with green and red accents – are indicative of colors available when the home was first built.

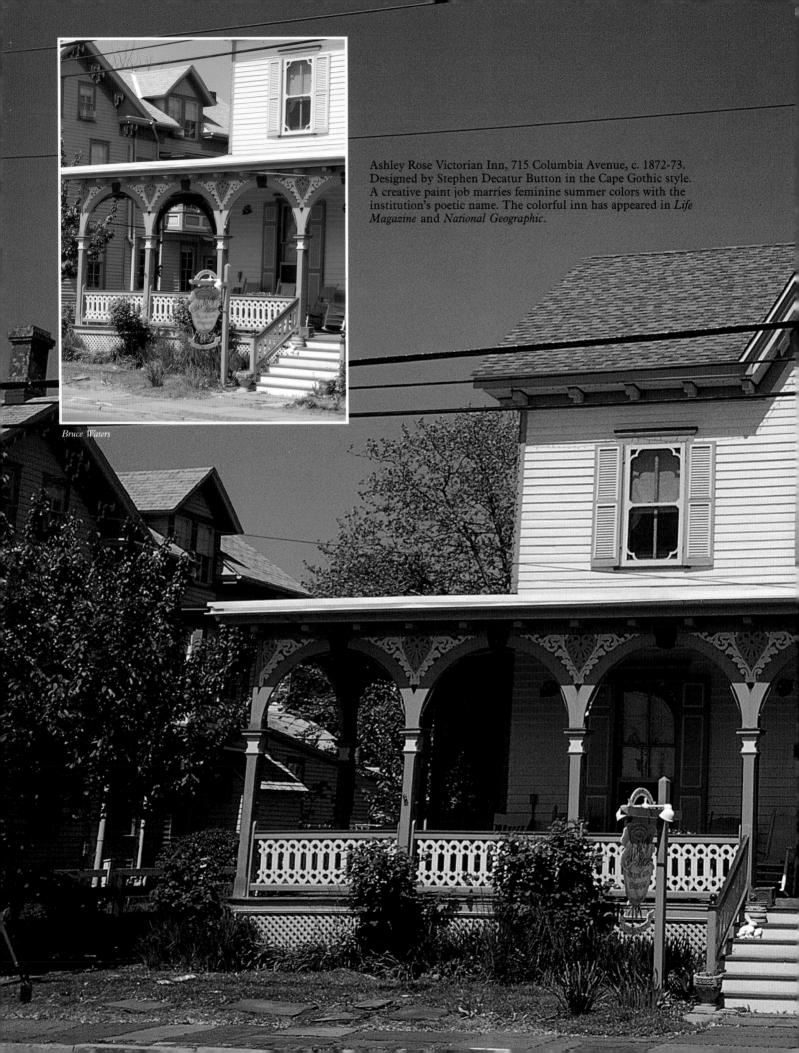

Ashley Rose Victorian Inn, 715 Columbia Avenue, c. 1872-73.
Designed by Stephen Decatur Button in the Cape Gothic style.
A creative paint job marries feminine summer colors with the
institution's poetic name. The colorful inn has appeared in *Life
Magazine* and *National Geographic*.

Bruce Waters

Bruce Waters

Bruce Waters

Bruce Waters

Bruce Waters

8

Mainstay Inn, 635 Columbia Avenue, c. 1872. Italianate Villa with a sweeping veranda and a cupola, designed by Stephen Decatur Button in a style reminiscent of antebellum architecture. Originally built as a gambling and entertainment club for gentlemen, it later housed distinguished naval officers and their families stationed in Cape May during World War I. The Mainstay Inn has been featured in *Architectural Digest*, *Travel and Leisure*, and *The New York Times*, among many others.

Delsea Hotel, 621 Columbia Avenue, c. 1867. Candy cane Corinthian columns and dental molding are among the finer details of gingerbread appliqués on this historic cottage.

The Abbey, 34 Gurney Street, c. 1869-70. The sixty-foot tower makes this home a standout in the city. It is Gothic Revival style, typified by steeply pitched roofs, hood molds over the windows, and the curvilinear gingerbread trim along the eaves and gable edges. Designed by Stephen Decatur Button for a wealthy coal baron as his summer home.

Tina Skinner

The Mason Cottage Bed & Breakfast, 625 Columbia Avenue, c. 1871. Built as a private summer residence by Edward A. Warne, a wealthy Philadelphia entrepreneur. The Warne family sold the "cottage" to the Mason family in the mid-1940s. The Mason's have maintained the building's original shade of off-white and even restored much of the original furniture. Mauve and a rich shade of green are used to highlight the bric-a-brac woodwork, and the windows are trimmed in a traditional dark red.

The Stockton Cottages, or Stockton Place Row Houses, Gurney Street. Gothic Revival cottages originally built as rentals in 1869. The Stockton Row cottages were a summer retreat for wealthy families who, together with their servants and nannies, would travel from Philadelphia and Virginia to summer in Cape May. (Details on following pages.)

Bruce Waters

Bruce Waters

Bruce Waters

Bruce Waters

Bruce Waters

The Belvidere, a private residence, 26 Gurney Street. One of The Stockton Cottages, originally built as rentals in 1869.

John Wesley Inn, 30 Gurney Street, c. 1869. Carpenter Gothic restored precisely to its original condition by the Tice family, owners since 1983.

22 Gurney Street. One of The Stockton Cottages.

The Gingerbread House, 28 Gurney Street, c. 1869. Owners Fred and Joan Echevarria have lovingly restored their Victorian home and bed and breakfast.

Tina Skinner

18

Tina Skinner

Tina Skinner

Tina Skinner

24 Gurney Street. One of The Stockton Cottages.

Tina Skinner

Tina Skinner

Top left: 20 Gurney Street. One of The Stockton Cottages.

Top right: 18 Gurney Street. One of The Stockton Cottages.

Bottom right: 16 Gurney Street. One of The Stockton Cottages.

Tina Skinner

Tina Skinner

839 Kearney Avenue. This classic Second Empire style home is topped by a Mansard roof, and prettied by the curve of a veranda and arched accent windows.

Mooring Guest House, 801 Stockton Avenue, 1882. One of Cape May's few bed and breakfast inns originally built as a guesthouse, designed to accommodate the fashionable Victorian on seaside holiday.

Summer Cottage Inn, 613 Columbia Avenue, c. 1867. Commissioned to be built by S. A. Harrison as a family summer vacation cottage. Philadelphia Architect Stephen Decatur Button created this Italianate style home complete with cupola.

Tina Skinner

The Stockton Manor, 805 Beach Drive, c. 1872-73. Classic Second Empire style is apparent in the original block of the structure, with a mere suggestion of a protruding central pavilion. Later add-ons include a wrap-around veranda and additions to the rear.

Morning Star Villa, 1307 Beach Drive, c. 1884-85. A star motif is repeated in moldings and gingerbread applications. But for the fourth floor, a later edition, this home is classic Second Empire style.

Opposite page: Joseph Leedom House, Congress and Lafayette Streets, c. 1887. Queen Anne style typified by asymmetrical massing of various architectural elements and a mix of finishes. A pair of towers adds impressive stature to a home, with unexpected dormers and porches adding interest and variety throughout the structure.

805 Stockton Avenue. "Mother Daughter" twin home, built in 1881.

902 Washington Street. Pink, white, and picket fence typify the charm and allure of rural Victorian architecture.

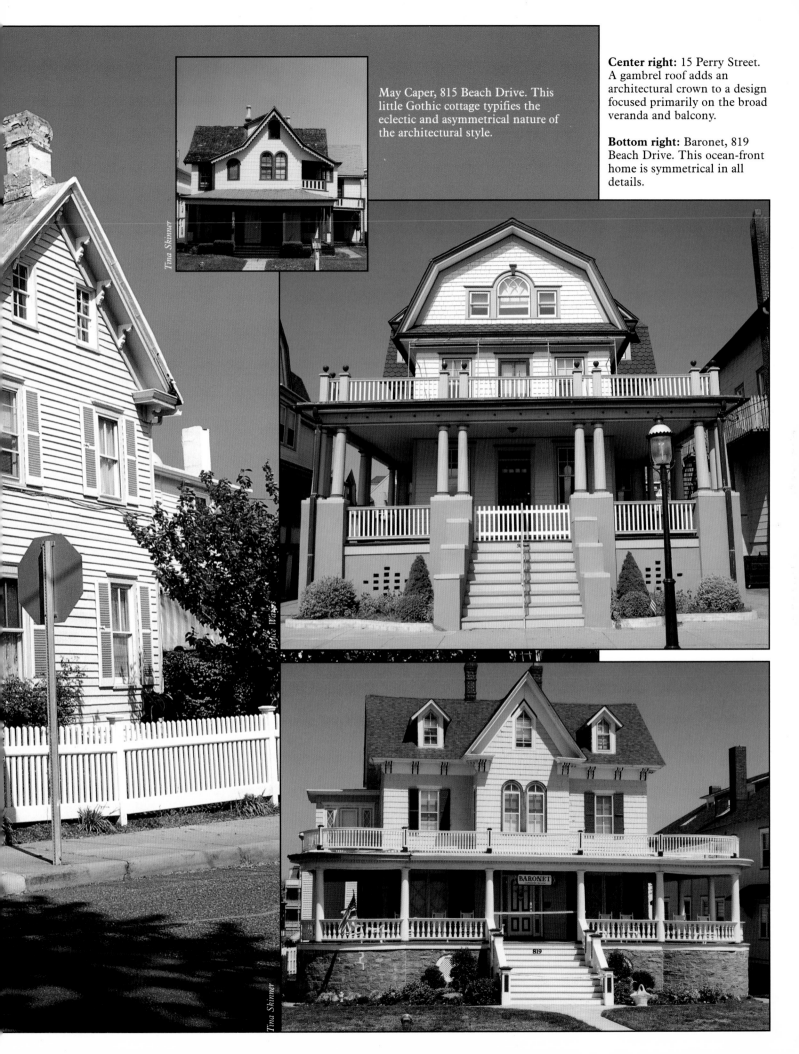

May Caper, 815 Beach Drive. This little Gothic cottage typifies the eclectic and asymmetrical nature of the architectural style.

Tina Skinner

Center right: 15 Perry Street. A gambrel roof adds an architectural crown to a design focused primarily on the broad veranda and balcony.

Bottom right: Baronet, 819 Beach Drive. This ocean-front home is symmetrical in all details.

Bruce Waters

Tina Skinner

BARONET

819

921 Beach Drive. Bric-a-brac and turned rails adorn this ocean-front property.

931 Beach Drive. Seemingly in search of Second Empire style, with the Mansard roof and a projecting central pavilion, this building strayed from symmetry with the addition of a three-story tower.

Tina Skinner

Cape Scape, 933 Beach Drive. A conical roof accentuates and unusual top line in this eclectic, ocean-front property.

Tina Skinner

The Inn on the Ocean, E.D. Wolfe Cottage, 25 Ocean Street, c. 1880. Intricate cutout work on the railings and roof cresting are among the pretty details on this French Second Empire cottage. The pink fish-scale siding adds icing to the bracketed, straight mansard roof.

Tina Skinner

Tina Skinner

Bruce Waters

606 Columbia Avenue. Built by the same millionaire who commissioned the Abbey, this modest home served as summer getaway for his son. The home's elaborate railings and wrought iron roof work captivate the eye.

Bruce Waters

Beauclaire's, 23 Ocean Street, c. 1879. Built after the fire of 1878, this is classic Queen Anne style – asymmetrical with a medley of architectural elements including a conical roof over the tower and an encircling veranda. Five original leaded glass windows are a true treat. Wallis Warfield, later the Duchess of Windsor, summered here according to local lore.

Bruce Waters

Bruce Waters

Tina Skinner

Tina Skinner

The Empress, formerly Bell Shields House, Decatur and Hughes Streets. Pretty colors and the sheer immensity of this stick style dwelling leave a lasting impression.

Tina Skinner

Bruce Waters

Tina Skinner

Tina Skinner

The Christopher Gallagher House, 45 Jackson Street, c. 1882-83. Identical to Poor Richard's Inn (following) with an extended porch. The Second Empire style emphasizes perfect symmetry at each of the three levels.

Poor Richard's Inn, 17 Jackson Street, c. 1882. Perfect example of Second Empire, with mansard roof and exacting symmetry. Restoration work included replacement of 1,600 pieces of multi-colored roof slate.

Top left: Abigail Adams Bed and Breakfast, 12 Jackson Street. One of the Seven Sisters

Center left: 18 Jackson Street. Detailing and color help keep one of the Seven Sisters in line with the rest of Cape May's fanciful Victorians.

Top right: The Seven Sisters, 10-20 Jackson Street, c. 1891-92. These seven identical homes actually open to a private courtyard (Atlantic Terrace) and were designed by Stephen Decatur Button on the site of The Atlantic Hotel, a victim of the great fire of 1878. These tightly contained cubes are typical of Renaissance Revival, imitating sixteenth century urban Italian homes. However, light gingerbread and molding applications are more typical of the town than the architectural form.

Bottom right: 45 Jackson Street. A towering Second Empire leaves no one guessing with its greatly projected central pavilion, in this case used as porch and balcony.

Tina Skinner

209 Perry Street. Pretty pink and white mingle with shingle under a distinctive gambrel roof.

206 Perry Street. An enclosed porch retained its gingerbread treatment above and below.

Opposite page: 33 Perry Street. An appropriately pink bridal shop, Uniquely Yours, is located on the first floor of this elaborately trimmed, three-tiered "wedding cake" of a Gothic Revival house. Naturally, the business specializes in Victorian weddings.

44

The Merry Widow, formerly J. Henry Edmonds House, 42 Jackson Street, c. 1879. The curved porch accentuates the curve of the building's tower, built-in to the straight mansard roofline of a modified Queen Anne castle-ette. The witch's hat tower cap presents a fanciful front-on view.

The King's Cottage, 9 Perry Street, c. 1879. This stick-style cottage was designed by Philadelphia architect Frank Furness. The detail image shows ceramic tiles, which were part of the Japanese exhibition from the Philadelphia Centennial of 1876.

Door detail from 216 Perry Street. Eggplant purple and white make wonderful accent colors.

Tina Skinner

Tina Skinner

Door details from The Parris Inn, 204 Perry Street.

Tina Skinner

213 Perry Street. An artist was inspired to paint leaves on the front stair risers of this pretty, Gothic cottage.

Tina Skinner

Opposite page: The Albert Stevens Inn, 127 Myrtle Avenue, 1898 Queen Anne Victorian home. Commissioned as a wedding gift by Dr. Albert G. Stevens, a Cape May homeopathic medical doctor, for his bride, Bessie. The house was restored and converted to a bed and breakfast inn in 1980 when Vesta Stevens-Olsen, the only child of Albert and Bessie died and the house was sold to investors.

Bruce Waters

Southern Mansion, 700 Washington Street, 1863. Philadelphia industrialist George Allen commissioned this American bracket, post and beam villa on Cape May, designed by the internationally acclaimed architect Samuel Sloan and constructed by Henri Phillipi. Allen and his descendants used this country estate for the next eighty-three years. It was then converted to a boarding house following its sale in the 1940s, after which it fell into incredible squalor and disrepair. It is the largest and most opulent Cape May mansion, in the heart of the historic district. The estate was restored and reopened in 1996, including two acres of award-winning gardens.

Tina Skinner

John F. Craig House, 609 Columbia Avenue, Carpenter Gothic style inn.

Opposite page: 908 Stockton Avenue. Red fish-scale shingles and gingerbread trim adorn this simple cottage.

The Belmont, 712 Columbia Avenue, c. 1879. A polygonal chimney is one of the hallmarks of the Gothic Revival cottage, along with embellished hooded dormers in the steeply pitched roofs. In a town where most cottages have been retrofit with retractable awnings, this permanent awning has obvious advantages.

Bruce Waters

Dormer House, 800 Columbia Avenue at Franklin, c. 1899.

The Henry Sawyer Inn, 722 Columbia Avenue, c. 1877. This gable-roofed cottage owes its existence to two of the town's most prominent historical figures. The building was commissioned by Eldridge Johnson – treasurer of Cape May, president of the Cape May Savings and Building Association, and trustee of the Presbyterian Church; and built by Henry Sawyer – Cape May's Civil War hero, proprietor of the Chalfonte Hotel, and Cape May city councilman. Johnson lived in this home for thirty-three years. A plaque on the inn commemorates Mr. Johnson and his public service to the town.

Bruce Waters

Belvedere Condos, 101 Lafayette Street. Accent colors highlight the brackets and ornaments on this spacious Italianate style home.

Bruce Waters

601 Columbia Avenue. This is one of the few remaining original Victorian storefronts in Cape May.

Tina Skinner

Tina Skinner

670 Welsh Street, Prickly Pear Cottage. This pretty Queen Anne style cottage is home to The Art League in Cape May. Two three-sided dormers add architectural interest to the building.

LOCAL FINE ART

Tina Skinner

The Queen Victoria Bed & Breakfast, 102 Ocean Street, c. 1881. An imposing block of building, this Second Empire style home is made graceful by the bell curves of the mansard roof, accentuated by a green and red color palette.

The Joseph Hall House, 645 Hughes Street, c. 1868. A striking color combination highlights the intricate vergeboard.

Franklin Hughes House, 665 Hughes Street. Wisteria softens the façade of this gaily painted, Gothic Revival private residence.

Bruce Waters

Bruce Waters

Bruce Waters

Bruce Waters

203 Congress Place. This Italianate mansion presents a formidable three-floor front to passersby.

130-132 Decatur Street. Pretty houses, all in a row, present a colorful front.

Sugar Plum Cottage, 114 Decatur Street. The most expressively colorful home in Cape May, this one is like-named, as well.

Tina Skinner

Tina Skinner

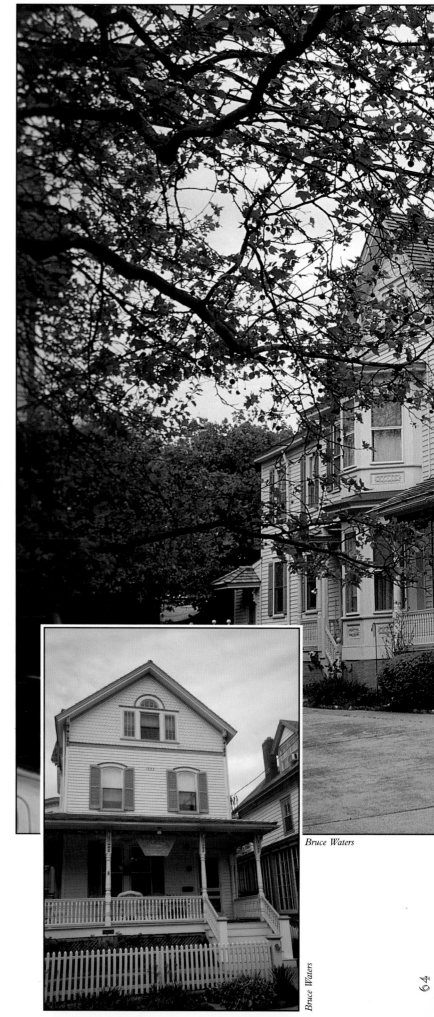

Bruce Waters

Bruce Waters

64

The Goodman House, 118 Decatur Street. A dollhouse and miniature museum occupy this happy blue and yellow themed Victorian. Next door, pink and white make a pretty partnership.

Opposite page
Top left: 130 Decatur Street, c. 1895. A prominent brow or arch over this window, and a tower with pyramidal roof are among the architectural features that distinguish this small domicile.

Bottom left: 124 Decatur Street. A snug yellow Second Empire home is iced with olive and brick red trim.

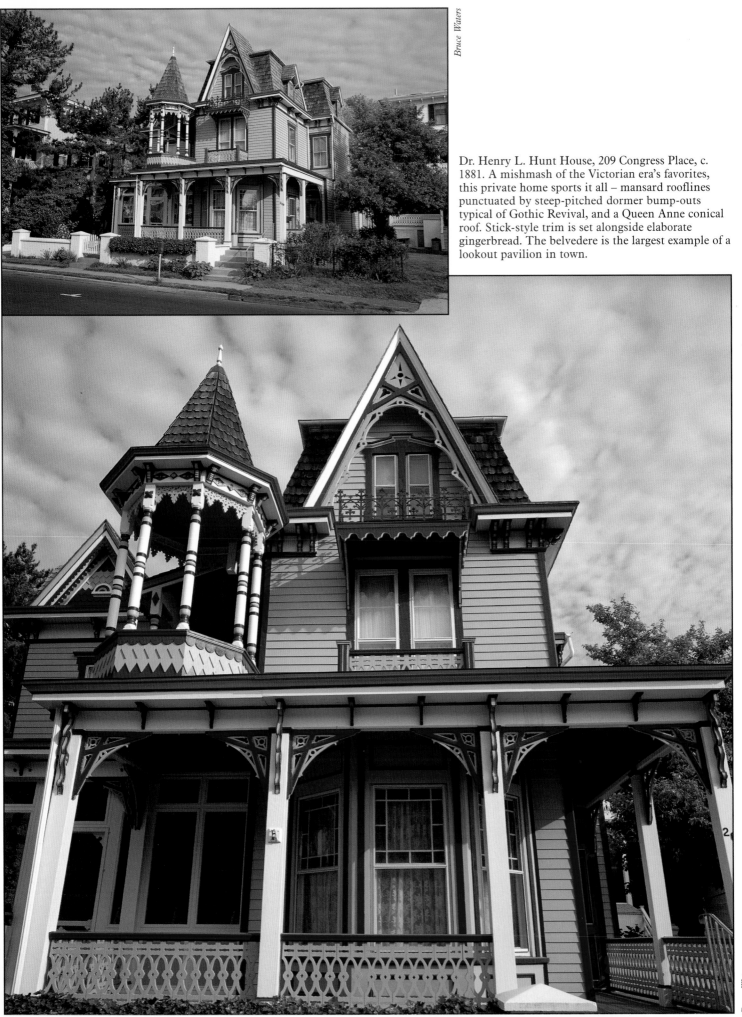

Dr. Henry L. Hunt House, 209 Congress Place, c. 1881. A mishmash of the Victorian era's favorites, this private home sports it all – mansard rooflines punctuated by steep-pitched dormer bump-outs typical of Gothic Revival, and a Queen Anne conical roof. Stick-style trim is set alongside elaborate gingerbread. The belvedere is the largest example of a lookout pavilion in town.

Judson Bennett House, 835 Washington Street, c. 1882. A jaunty tower and second floor overhangs add to the architectural variety of a Queen Anne style home.

Bruce Waters

Tina Skinner

Inn at 22 Jackson Street, c. 1899. A flashy coat of paint brings out the best in this feature-packed Queen Anne style home. Exterior assets include clusters of elaborate turned porch columns and a jaunty octagonal tower topped by a "witch's hat" conical roof.

210 Congress Street. Steep roof angles belie the rounded face this residence presents to passersby.

Tina Skinner

Tina Skinner

Chalfonte Hotel, Howard and Sewell Streets, c. 1876. American Bracketed Villa with Italianate decorative elements. Civil War hero Colonel Henry Sawyer may have fought for the North, but the hotel he built and operated exudes Southern charm and hospitality.

Captain Mey's Bed and Breakfast, formerly Dr. Walter H. Philips House, 202 Ocean Street, c. 1890. Colonial Revival named for the first foreign explorer to visit the area – Capt. Cornelius Jacobsen Mey of Holland. Mey declared the regional climate as good as his homeland's and named Cape May for himself.

Tina Skinner

613 Columbia Avenue, and Pharo's, 617 Columbia Avenue, designed by Stephen Decatur Button. These two matching Italianate buildings make a pretty pair, their differences a point of contemplation from the street.

Bruce Waters

The Inn of Cape May, Beach Drive and Ocean Street, c. 1894. This imposing Queen Ann style hotel is crowned by twin tent roofs. In 1917, Wallis Warfield, later the Duchess of Windsor, had her "coming out" party here.

Angel of the Sea Inn, 5-7 Trenton Street, c. 1850. Built as a "summer cottage" for Philadelphia chemist William Weightman, Sr., this was originally a single building that stood on the corner of Franklin and Washington Streets until 1881, when Mr. Weightman's son decided he wanted an ocean. Local farmers, who were hired to move the house to the corner of Ocean and Beach avenues, discovered the house was too large to move as one unit, so they cut it in half, and spent the better part of the winter pulling the sections on rolling tree trunks with mule and horse power! Unfortunately, after both halves arrived, the farmers discovered that their pulling animals were ineffective in "pushing" it back together. With the owners due to arrive back soon, the farmers enclosed the sides where the cut had been made, renovated as best they could, and hurried back to their farming chores. The two buildings were moved again in 1962 to make room for a hotel, carried this time on flatbed trucks. Subsequent neglect, followed by a massive renovation in the 1980s, earned the Angel an award from the National Trust for Historic Preservation in Washington, DC for renovation to historic specifications.

Bruce Waters

Bruce Waters

The Linda Lee Bed and Breakfast, formerly the John Benezet Cottage, 725 Columbia Avenue, c. 1872. A pair of pointed windows are central gems on this Carpenter Gothic.

Bruce Waters

701 Columbia Avenue. Shingle style, though not a standout in a town of painted gingerbread, was one of the Victorian Era mainstays in cottage construction and continues in popularity today.

Leith Hall, 22 Ocean Street. This Second Empire wears a wonderful striped-awning skirt.

Celtic Inn, 24 Ocean Street. A small Second Empire has a new life as a bed and breakfast.

Bruce Waters

107 Ocean Street. Fish-scale shingles and clapboard add variety to a classic Gothic cottage.

Bruce Waters

Bruce Waters

Fairthorne Cottage Bed and Breakfast, 111 Ocean Street. A Queen Anne style home, this cottage now doubles as an inn with the house next door.

The Fairthorne Bed and Breakfast, 115 Ocean Street. This Colonial Revival was built by a whaling captain in 1892.

Bruce Waters

INDEX

Abbey, The 11, 34

Abigail Adams Bed and Breakfast 41

Albert Stevens Inn 48

Angel of the Sea Inn 74, 75

Ashley Rose Victorian Inn 6, 7

Atlantic Hotel, The 41

Atlantic Terrace 41

Baronet 31

Beach Drive 26, 31, 32, 33, 73, 74

Beauclaire's 35

Bell Shields House 36, 37

Belvidere, The 17

Brass Bed Inn 5

Belmont, The 54

Belvedere Condos 56

Button, Stephen Decatur 4, 6, 11, 25, 41, 72

Cape Scape 33

Captain Mey's Bed and Breakfast 71

Celtic Inn 78

Chalfonte Hotel 70, 71

Christopher Gallagher House 38, 39

Columbia Avenue 5, 6, 9, 10, 12, 13, 24, 25, 34, 52, 54, 55, 56, 57, 72, 76, 77

Congress Place 63, 66

Congress Street 29

Decatur Street 36, 37, 62, 63, 64, 65

Delsea Hotel 10

Dormer House 54, 55

Dr. Henry L. Hunt House 66

Dr. Walter H. Philips House 71

E.D. Wolfe Cottage 33

Empress, The 36, 37

Fairthorne Cottage Bed and Breakfast 79

Franklin Hughes House 61

Franklin Street 55, 74

Furness, Frank 4, 46

Gingerbread House 18, 19

Goodman House, The 65

Gurney Street 11, 14, 15, 16, 17, 18, 19, 20, 21

Henry Sawyer Inn 56

Howard Street 70

Hughes Street 36, 37, 60, 61

Inn at 22 Jackson Street 68, 69

Inn of Cape May 73

Inn on the Ocean 33

J. Henry Edmonds House 45

Jackson Street 38, 39, 40, 41, 44, 45, 60, 69

John F. Craig House 52

Johnson, Eldridge 56

John Benezet Cottage 76

John Wesley Inn 16, 17

Joseph Hall House 60

Joseph Leedom House 29

Judson Bennett House 67

Kearney Avenue 4, 23

King's Cottage, The 46

Lafayette Street 29, 56

Leith Hall 77

Linda Lee Bed and Breakfast 76

Mainstay Inn 8, 9

Mason Cottage 12, 13

May Caper 31

Merry Widow, The 44, 45

Mey, Capt. Cornelius Jacobsen 71

Mooring Guest House 22, 23

Morning Star Villa 26

Myrtle Avenue 49

Ocean Street 33, 35, 59, 71, 73, 74, 77, 78, 79

Parris Inn 47

Perry Street 31, 42, 43, 46, 47, 49

Pharo's 72

Phillipi, Henri 50

Poor Richard's Inn 39, 40

Prickly Pear Cottage 58

Queen Victoria Bed & Breakfast 59

Sawyer, Henry 56

Sea Mist, The 5

Seven Sisters, The 41

Sewell Street 70

Sloan, Samuel 4, 50

Southern Mansion 50, 51

Stockton Avenue 22, 23, 27, 53

Stockton Cottage 14, 15, 17, 20, 21

Stockton Manor, The 27

Stockton Place Row Houses 14, 15

Sugar Plum Cottage 62

Summer Cottage Inn 24, 25

Trenton Street 74

Uniquely Yours 42

Washington Street 30, 31, 50, 51, 67, 74

Weightman, William 74

Welsh Street 58